THE MEN'S GARMENT INDUSTRY OF NEW YORK AND THE STRIKE OF 1913

BY
HARRY BEST, Ph.D.

UNIVERSITY SETTLEMENT STUDIES
UNIVERSITY SETTLEMENT SOCIETY
NEW YORK

PRICE 25 CENTS

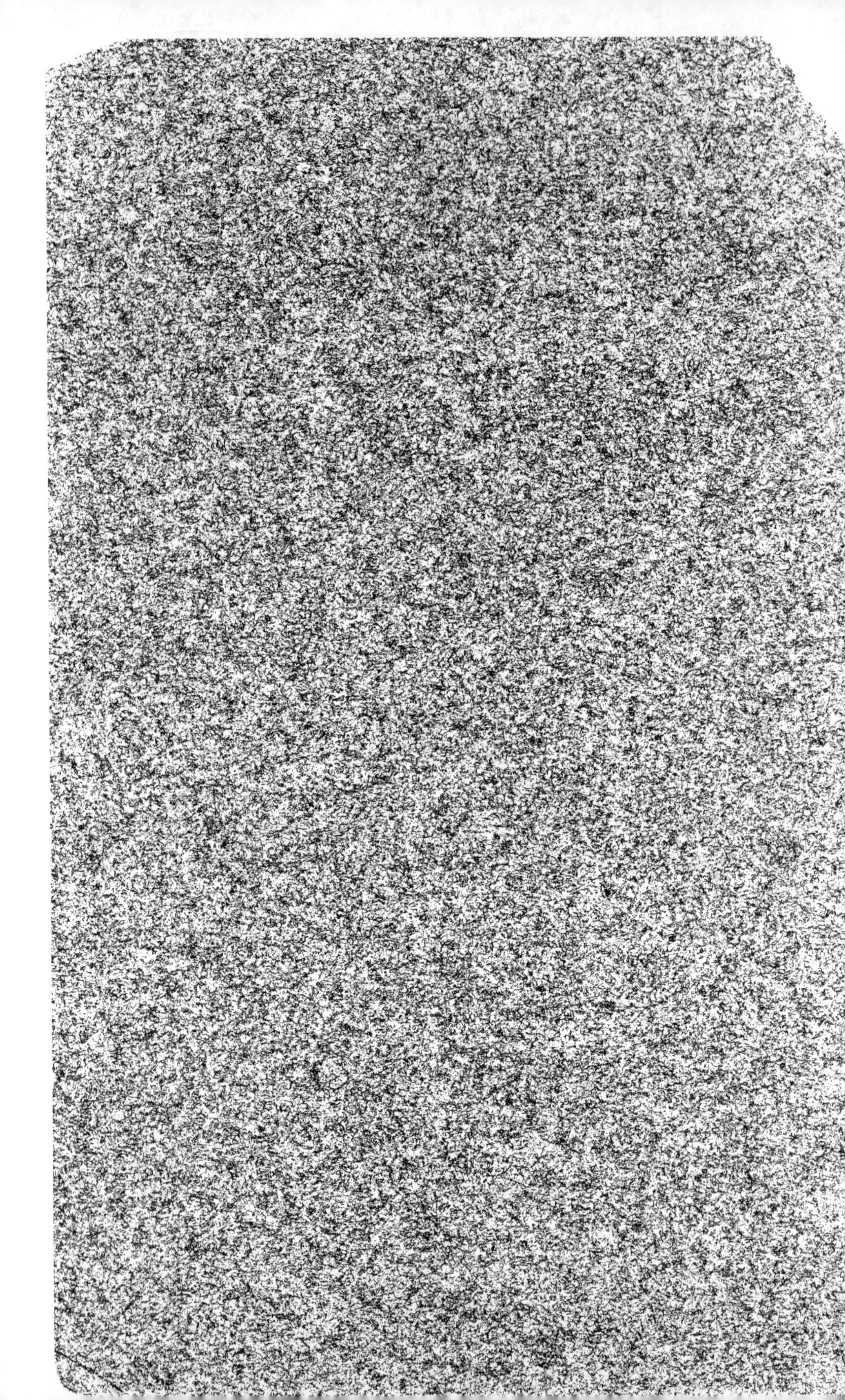

THE MEN'S GARMENT INDUSTRY OF NEW YORK AND THE STRIKE OF 1913

BY

HARRY BEST, Ph.D.

UNIVERSITY SETTLEMENT STUDIES
UNIVERSITY SETTLEMENT SOCIETY
NEW YORK

PRICE 25 CENTS

THE MEN'S GARMENT INDUSTRY IN NEW YORK AND THE STRIKE OF 1913[1]

In the beginning of the year 1913 there occurred a strike in the clothing industry in New York which was notable for several things: the great number of persons involved; the immense losses resulting both to the workers and to the employers; and the unusual prolongation, both sides holding out to the limit of their endurance. The strike concerned an industry related closely to human comfort and necessity. It took place in what is really the seat of the industry. It had to do with a situation in no small measure affected by great inflowing streams of immigrant labor, and by the passing of an industry into the factory system. Such was the setting of the strike which we are now to consider.

The number of persons taking part in the men's garment strike was hardly under 100,000.[2] Other strikes in women's garment industries at the same time, though in no wise related to the main strike, swelled the total number to 150,000, and added to the public apprehension. The strike continued nearly nine weeks, and during this time hardly less than $7,000,000 was lost to the workers in wages[3]; the loss to the manufacturers, though it cannot be known, must have been tremendous; while no little was suffered by the clerks and others who worked in the establishments, and by landlords, grocers, and others who depended on the workers.

[1] The present study is based upon observations made at the time of the strike, and upon an examination of the trade and trade union journals, especially the *Garment Worker,* of New York, as well as of the New York daily newspapers. Other sources of information will be duly cited.

[2] By scarcely any of the New York newspapers was the number estimated at less than 85,000, while the union and Socialist papers put the number above 100,000.

[3] If the average wage of the men be taken as $13, and of the women as $8, the total loss for the nine weeks would be some ten million dollars. A certain proportion of the workers, however, returned to work within a shorter time, which reduces this figure.

With the numbers involved, and with the large issues at stake, it seemed quite possible that, should the workers win, their victory might result in the form of a protocol or preferential union shop, already secured two years before in the suit, cloak, and skirt strike. Such a victory would have been most important, and would have marked the greatest advance yet reached in labor contests. However, the workers were not to achieve such a result. The fight was waged so bitterly by the employers, and their resources proved so much the stronger that, though the workers made some very substantial gains, the fruits to them fell much short of what they had striven for.

To appreciate the full meaning of the strike, it will be necessary to examine both the past development and the present condition of the men's ready-made clothing industry in New York. That this industry has become an immense business in the city is fairly well known, but it is probable that few realize its full extent and importance. Its history is concerned not only with the rise and growth of a great business, but with the situation brought about by new processes of manufacture, and by the nature of a labor market resulting from great tidal waves of immigration, which have swept one race after another into the country, the newer pushing the older further up in the scale of employment.

Early in the nineteenth century New York began to be recognized as a clothing center, though ready-to-wear garments were then but little known. By 1840 the value of the industry was said to be $2,000,000. At the time of the Civil War it had reached nearly six million dollars, and there were some twenty thousand persons engaged in the industry. But it is in comparatively recent years that the greatest growth has been shown, being in this time hardly less than phenomenal. To-day the value of the industry in the city reaches several hundred million dollars, with nearly two hundred thousand workers in it.

Great as has the industry become in mere size, even more notable has been the change in the racial character of the workers. It is quite possible that there is no other industry in America which indicates so clearly the effects of our immigration policy.

At the beginning of the industry it was in the hands of

purely native stock, reinforced by English and Scotch kinsmen from across the sea. Towards the middle of the century the Irish and the Germans began to enter, for a time the latter seeming to be about to take possession of the field. However, it was another race that was destined to obtain the mastery. In the '70's and '80's, especially in the latter period, owing to conditions in Russia, the Jews had begun to seek America in great numbers, though before this they had been trickling in. They gathered in New York, and with the clothing industry growing as it was, they were not long in making entry into it. Beginning in considerable measure as merchants in second-hand clothing, they passed readily into the business of manufacturers. As their immigration increased, they began to supplant other races, and the industry came more and more into their hands. In time not only did they furnish the bulk of the workers, but the control of the industry came almost entirely to be turned over to them. Indeed, had it not been for the further action of the forces of immigration, the industry might have become a distinctly racial one.

As time went on, other peoples of Europe followed the call to America. The one of these that stopped in New York in huge numbers was the Italian, and they too were destined to leave an impress upon the character of the industry. Their arrival took place mainly in the late '80's and the '90's, and it was their women mostly who came in to underbid the Jews, their chief part being played in the taking of the goods to the home to be finished. Yet, nothwithstanding this, the direction of the industry has remained with the Jews, and it is they who are so largely associated with it. They now almost completely own the shops; while of those who are still workers it is the consuming ambition to become contractors to some manufacturer, and with this as a stepping stone to become regular employers.

Parallel with the changes in the racial constitution of the workers in the industry have been changes in the processes of production. Before the middle of the nineteenth century there was a little ready-made clothing on the market, to be purchased at about half the price of custom made. The manufacture of this took place in the homes, where it remained for many years, the introduction of the system being largely due to the Germans. Under this arrangement the head of the house had for his working force his wife and family, with an occasional outsider. The sewing machine had now come into use, and this added greatly to efficiency of production. Yet prior to the Civil War the amount of ready-made clothing manufactured was not large.

With the entry of the Jews into the industry, there commenced a new epoch in the processes of manufacture. The industry was now being greatly extended, and they came in when a system known as the contract system was being fixed. Between the years 1876 and 1882 the "task system" forced its way into the industry, which was dependent upon a "team" or "set" of workers. Such a combination consisted of three persons, whose duties were rather sharply separated: a baster, an operator, and a finisher, the last being usually a girl. When first inaugurated, a "task" was the completion of a given number of garments. As competition became keener, the number of garments constituting a "task" was increased, without, however, effecting a corresponding increase in pay. For instance, at one time the making of 8 or 9 coats formed a task, but later the number was forced up to 11 or 12. It was at this point mainly that the door was opened for the introduction of the sweating system, which has since been associated with the making of clothing. In this process the journeyman tailor had to abandon the field, and the hiring of regular operatives became the order. Under such an arrangement the Jew began to occupy the field, and it was here that he displayed his wonderful and relentless energy, it being his overmastering desire to have an establishment at some time of his own.

The next stage in the course of manufacture was the introduction into the industry of the factory system, which came from Boston. This is the system to-day employed, though home work is still carried on to a greater or less extent. Such has been the development up to the present, briefly told, of the men's ready-made garment industry in New York. The present organization of the industry requires a somewhat closer examination.[4]

---

[4] Very valuable accounts of the development of the clothing industry in New York are found in the studies of Dr. Jesse E. Pope, "The Clothing Industry in New York", 1905 (University of Missouri Studies), and Mrs. E. E. Willett, "Employment of Women in the

In the present arrangement of the industry the work of manufacture is really done in three separate and distinct places: in the factory itself, in the shop of a contractor, and in the home of the worker. In some cases practically all the operations are performed in the factory, that is, in an "inside shop", which is especially likely to be true in the case of better grade garments; but such an arrangement is found in but a small portion of the industry. The vast amount of the work, perhaps nine-tenths, is partly completed in the factory, and then is given to the contractor to be finished, a portion of this passing to the homes for certain minor operations. To-day in the making of a suit of clothes the division of labor is carried to a far degree. A garment requires many different operations, a pocket, for instance, having alone several distinct ones. In a full suit of clothes as many as a hundred workers may have had some part. The greatest division of labor is found in the better grade of goods.

The manufacturers of ready-made clothing in general buy the cloth and trimming in large quantities from some special factory or jobber, and have it brought into their establishments. Here it is cut into the required patterns for the garments that are to be made up. This work is done by the cutters, all of whom work in the regular factory. They are the most skilled workers, and their work is the most important in the industry, having to do with the finer points in shaping a garment according to the prevailing styles or demands. They are paid the highest wages, and are often referred to as the "aristocrats" of the trade. They in fact form a distinct group in the business, and have not always come in very close touch with the workers in the scale below them. In the regular establishments there are also trimmers and examiners, the latter seeing that the garments, whether completed in the factory or outside, are properly made. There are in addition in most shops a certain number of pressers. In large establishments the total number of men may be several hundred, in a few approaching a thousand; but in most it is less than a hundred.

The cloth, having been attended to by the cutters, is now ready for the contractor. This person plays a highly important

Clothing Trades", 1902 (Columbia University Studies in History, Economics, and Public Law.).

part in the industry. It is he who deals directly with the men, the real "tailors", the nominal manufacturer rarely coming in contact with them. Sometimes he has one or more subcontractors working under him. His specialty is in one particular garment, as the coat, the pants or the vest, for it is to be remembered that the three pieces of a suit of clothes are manufactured separately. One contractor takes the coat, another the vest, and the third the pants. All the parts are reassembled by the manufacturer if he desires a full suit. Sometimes in a large establishment a considerable number of contractors are dealt with.

The contractor takes his article, and agrees to return it at a certain time. For the work he proposes to do upon it, no great amount of capital is needed. His floor space does not need to be large, and every square inch is made to count. Equipped with needle, shears, sewing machine, and pressing iron, he is ready to begin work. A typical task shop under him will consist of three teams (each having a baster, an operator, and a finisher), two pressers, a button-sewer and pocket tacker, and, in addition, several other persons, chiefly women, who are engaged in such work as felling and the like. A subcontractor is usually engaged to make machine button-holes, while the pads necessary in certain parts of garments can be procured at special shops. The contractor during all this is proving himself something more than "boss". He seldom spares himself, and is found to be one of the hardest and most efficient workers in the place. He is chiefly employed at lining and bushelling, that is, general remodelling or repairing.

The contractor is not to be despised, nor is he to be altogether condemned. His rôle is very different from that of the ordinary middleman. It is he who first meets the raw immigrant laborer, provides him with a job, and gives him an introduction to American ways. The opportunities he has are thus great for service both to the worker and to the community at large. The principle of contracting is itself not bad, but is quite legitimate, and may be a necessary and essential part in the manufacture of a great article of human consumption. Yet in such a situation there lies no little danger. The main trouble is in the want of responsibility of the contractor. The worker is usually quite at his mercy. Often cut-throat competition exists, and the contractor can only continue in business by making further exactions upon his help. The workers being new in the country, ignorant of other means of getting a living, and willing to accept the lowest wages and longest hours, are entirely within his power. They are thus unable to protest, and may be driven to the last extremity.

Home work, that is, the taking of goods to tenement homes for certain processes, has long been recognized as part of the garment industry. Probably it really amounts to less than is the usual belief, but that it is considerable is beyond question. It is mainly the Italian women that come for this work, many of whom live only a few blocks from the shops. In the performance of their tasks no great amount of skill is required. Their work consists mostly in felling, that is, stitching the lining to the coat, sewing around armholes, sewing on collars and cuffs, basting pants, sewing on buttons, tacking pockets, etc.

That home work is fraught with possibilities of great abuse, is evident; but how far the evils do exist is a matter difficult to ascertain. Dr. Jesse E. Pope in his study, "The Clothing Industry in New York",[5] does not believe that they are as great as is usually supposed. After speaking of the instances which from time to time arouse public indignation, he says: "It is these sporadic cases that the press and sensational writers are constantly exploiting." At the same time it is not to be denied that by the homework a means of small earnings is provided, the absence of which would prove a bitter hardship to those who live by it. Nevertheless, perhaps in the long run it would be better if home work were eliminated, and the community would be the gainer without it. The whole matter should be considered in plans for regulating immigration. At any rate, there is a decided call for the regulation of the system as it is. There is at present a certain amount of legal requirements as to home work, but of neither great extent nor effectiveness. In 1892 a law was enacted declaring work in the homes to be illegal when done by workers outside the family in rooms where there was eating or sleeping, and even here to be authorized only by permit of the board of health. In 1899 it was required that there be 500 cubit feet of air space for each worker, and that inspection be made every six months. There

[5] Page 161. Home work is also well described in the Report on the Condition of Woman and Child Wage-earners in the United States, 1910, vol. II.

are enumerated 41 articles which may be made in tenement houses, but the actual number so made is near 100. Oversight is given to the departments of health, labor, and tenements. In 1912 a law was enacted, requiring that on such goods there should be placed a label, "tenement made."

In the industry women have been employed from the start, but they are probably now in larger numbers than ever before. In regular factories they are found the least, in contractors' shops in greater proportions, and in home work practically altogether. In New York, according to the special census of manufactures of 1905, the number of women is relatively less than in the country generally. In the former the ratio is 61 per cent men to 39 per cent women, and in the latter 55 to 45. That is, in New York nearly two-fifths of the workers in the men's ready-made clothing industry are women. Just how far this includes tenement house workers cannot be known, though it seems doubtful if all could have been embraced.

We have thus far seen something of the processes of manufacture in the industry. It is now well for us to attempt to gain an insight into the general conditions of labor—from the point of view, that is, of the workers. These may be classified as the rate of wages, the hours of labor, and the sanitary surroundings. In respect to the rate of wages, it should be stated at the outset that the matter of obtaining schedules in respect to them is an exceedingly difficult one. The cutters are of course the highest paid, receiving, before the strike of 1913, in the best shops a maximum of something like $22 a week or more, but averaging less than $20. Below their grade wages vary considerably, ranging from $8 to $20, but averaging, it seems, $12 or $14. The wages of women appear to be from $5 to $11 in the shops, while in the homes $2 or $2.50 represents their earnings. For many persons the work is seasonal, and these are partly laid off several months a year, when they work but two or three days a week. According to the employers, the wages are fully ten per cent higher than in other cities.

As to hours of labor, we find the cutters again the most favored. Some have 48 hours, which has been the case for quite a few years, while others work 50, 52, 54, or 56 hours. For workers in the lower grades the hours are seldom under 54, and might extend to 60 or more. There has been a steady downward reduction of hours for a number of years. Women usually have the same hours as men, save as they have been modified by law. In homes the women have of course to give part of their time to household duties, but notwithstanding over half give six hours a day to their industrial work, and some much more.

In respect to sanitary conditions the shops present the widest range of difference. In some of the better class shops they are admitted to be good, and in a few they are excellent. It is in the cheaper shops in the poorer sections of the East Side that they are worst. These shops are frequently located in some old six or seven story building which has seen its best days. Unless on an upper floor the light is likely to be poor; wooden stairways are found more often than safety would allow; and filthy toilets are more common than not. In not a few shops over-crowding has reached a serious stage. The evils in home work have already been referred to. A thorough examination, however, would be necessary in order to determine the exact sanitary conditions of the entire industry.

A few words are now necessary in respect to the condition of the trade at the time of the strike. The growth of the trade in men's ready-made clothing has been truly remarkable, the demand for it having literally advanced by leaps and bounds. The industry now ranks seventh in gross value among manufactures in the United States, seventh in the number of wage-earners employed, and eighth in the amount of wages paid.[6] As a result, clothing is produced in far greater quantities than ever before. Not only this, but the price of such clothing is much lower than it was some years ago. A suit of a given quality costs less than half what it did two score years ago.

Although New York is the largest center of the industry in America, there are other cities where it is of considerable importance, notably Philadelphia, Boston, Baltimore, Chicago, Rochester, Cincinnati, and St. Louis. These constitute serious rivals, and the competing markets they afford play a large part in determining conditions in New York. This city retains its preëminence largely because of its position as an arbiter of styles, its position as a market for cheap immigrant labor, and its proximity to centers furnishing raw material. This in-

---

[6] See Special Reports on Manufactures, of the Census Bureau, 1905.

dustry ranks second in importance among the industries of the city, its value being over $300,000,000. Perhaps a third of a million people earn their living by the needle trades here, nearly half of whom are in the men's garment industry.

The men's ready-made clothing industry is confined not only to the usual suits of clothes, but includes dress suits, rain coats, smoking jackets, fancy vests, boys' clothing, sailor suits and similar garments. Children's ready-made clothing is perhaps concentrated in New York most of all, over three-fourths of the output being manufactured here. The products of the shops are sold everywhere in the United States, and also in many foreign lands. The better grade articles are often standard goods, many being well advertised.

In the city there are certain fairly defined areas for the clothing industry. The higher grade shops are located in Astor Place, upper Lafayette Street, Center Street, Broadway from Fourteenth to below Canal Street, with a number of cross streets. The lower grade shops are scattered over the district to the East and West, especially to the East, a number being on streets along the East River. In Williamsburg and in Brownsville on the Brooklyn side there are many shops also. The location of the industry in fact accounts in large part for the great congestion of population on the lower East Side of Manhattan Island, this district having a density equalled nowhere else in the world.

Thus far we have discussed the growth and present condition of the industry. Let us now see what is the condition of the workers, especially in the way of organization among themselves. The cutters were on the field early with their union, having organized in 1855. Since that time they have maintained a comparatively vigorous organization, and have been practically the only branch of the trade to develop strength up to recent times. For a number of years they showed little desire to have much to do with the others in the industry, the latter remaining a mass of unorganized workers for a long time. It was not an easy thing to organize them, because of the large and constant influx of immigrants, some 10,000 of them being said to be absorbed into the industry each year, especially in the children's jacket and boys' knee pants branches. Within the last decade, there has grown up a union of the tailors, including many of those below the grade of cutters, known as the Brotherhood of Tailors. It has sought the immigrant, and explained its objects to him, with the result that in time he comes to display a new attitude towards trade unionism. Many locals have now been established among the several branches of the trade, as the vest-makers, the pressers, the children's jacket-makers, etc. All are connected with the United Garment Workers of America, in affiliation with the American Federation of Labor.

With the organization of the industry, it was only a question of time till there should be strikes. These have taken place at various times, but for the most part have been small local affairs. In 1880 occurred the largest one up to that time, proving, however, unsuccessful. In 1893 there was another fairly large strike. This was at the time when the American Federation of Labor was making war upon the Knights of Labor. The coat tailors had demanded of the employers the discharge of all the workers belonging to the latter organization. Upon their refusal to do this, the men went on strike. Though defeated, the final result was the exclusion of their enemies. In 1895 a strike occurred in the clothing industry, which at first was believed to be a victory for the men, but was without any great permanent gain, except possibly that two years later a general agreement was entered into with the employers on certain matters. In the winter of 1901-1902 a strike was ordered for the New York locals of the United Garment Workers. Some 16,000 workers were called out, but the benefit to the union was little. In 1904 occurred the largest and most important strike so far in the industry, involving some 35,000 workers. It came from the action of the National Clothing Association in adopting a policy with respect to cutters and trimmers which seemed antagonistic to union principles. The strike lasted six weeks, and during it public sympathy was largely with the strikers. The men lost, however, due, it is said, to the strike's being ill-timed and its failure to include all the branches in the trade.

It might appear from this account that the unions of the United Garment Workers in New York were given to frequent strikes. This is not the case, however. As a matter of fact, the officials have exercised considerable caution in calling strikes. Both the local District Council and the General Executive Board have more than a few times laid a restraining hand upon attempted local action. This attitude, doubtless inspired in some measure by the results of strikes in the past, was apparent in the action of 1913; and there has been generally strong aversion to the calling of a strike until conditions have appeared propitious, and success seemed fairly certain. At the same time it must not be thought that the history of the strike movements has been a losing one. In several of them the men have gained some advantage, and in most the workers have become more conscious of the union spirit. One material gain has been in the use of the union label, which has been affixed to the garments manufactured in a number of houses, though as a matter of fact the public in its purchases has never displayed any marked interest in such labels.

We now come to the consideration of the strike of 1913. First, let us see what were the grievances of the workers that caused them to undergo the long period of unemployment and privation which they did. It may be said at the outset that there was no acute situation precipitating the strike. The strike might have occurred a year sooner or a year later, with little effect upon the actual matters involved. The industry had been quiet, so far as labor outbreaks were concerned, for nearly ten years. During this time it cannot be asserted that conditions had grown worse. There had been no new inventions introduced to which labor was hostile. The employers had taken no action that indicated unfriendliness to labor or to labor unions. No outstanding act of injustice or abuse was complained of.

Though it was sufficiently apparent that organizers had been busy in creating a sentiment for a strike among the workers for some time, it was none the less evident that this could not have taken place but with their hearty approval. The sentiment had been growing slowly for several years, and it was felt that it was only a question of time till the men should be called out. The strike was really due to the conviction that conditions in the trade, while not necessarily growing worse, were hardening, and that the effect in time would be disastrous to the men. Despite some improvements, it was a question with many whether, after all, their state might not be worse than it was before. At any rate it was felt that early action would have to be taken. An effective blow, they reasoned, must be struck before their predicament became intolerable.

As we have seen, the strike had been looked for and planned a year or more previously. In the summer and fall of 1912 evidences began to appear of the near approach of the strike. In October mass meetings of workers were held by a number of shops, to feel out the sense of the workers for immediate action. Early in November District Council No. 1 of the United Garment Workers of America, which has to do with New York, found the outlook so promising that appeals were issued to non-unionists to enlist in the approaching struggle. In all this there was encouragement from the national body.

Later in November a conference was held of representatives of the various locals, and the general sentiment was found to be for an early strike. On December 11 there were twenty-one mass meetings, attended by some 30,000 workers. Hopes were enkindled from the fact that now for the first time there seemed possible a strike of all the workers in the men's garment industry in all its branches, from the cutter down to the sewer of buttons. Furthermore, there was the vivid recollection of the battle two years before in the cloak, suit, and skirt industry. Had not the workers there after a prolonged and bitter struggle won a great victory and secured the protocol and preferential shop? Was it not possible that the same result might be attained here?

Formal voting on the proposition to strike began on December 18, and lasted till December 22. In it twenty-one branches of the garment-making industry took part. When the result was announced, it was found that 35,786 had voted for the strike, and 2,322 against it—a vote of 14 to 1 for the strike. According to the main branches of the trade, the vote was as follows:[7]

Branch	*For*	*Against*
Coat makers and allied trades of Manhattan........	21,058	743
Coat makers and allied trades of Brooklyn and Brownsville	3,754	308
Children's jacket makers	1,805	454
Pants makers of Greater New York	4,777	160
Vest makers of Greater New York	1,282	252
Button hole makers	312	22
Knee pants makers	2,000	243
Custom tailors	798	140
Total	35,786	2,322

[7] See *Garment Worker*, Dec. 13, 20, 27, 1912.

It is not to be supposed, however, that this number represented all who were to be affected by the strike. Only the members of the unions could vote, but it was hoped that by the strike the industry would be so tied up that non-unionists would be forced to leave their work, with the possibility of many coming over bodily into the union. The number that were expected to respond at once to the call were estimated at a little under 100,000, divided somewhat as follows:

Brotherhood of tailors	25,000
Vest makers	12,000
Pants makers union	12,000
Pressers union	10,000
Cutters union	8,000
Custom tailors	6,000
Overcoat and coat makers	5,000
Button hole makers	4,000
Children's jacket makers	3,000
Knee pants makers union	2,500
Boys' reefer suit makers union	2,500
Unbasted children's jacket makers	2,000
Lithuanian tailors union	2,000

Accordingly, the strike was called to take place on the last day of the old year, it being believed that the business would be hardest hit at this period.

In this strike the chief, or even overshadowing, demand was for an increase in wages. It was contended that for ten years there had been practically no increase, while the cost of living had constantly mounted upward. As a further basis for this demand, it was claimed that the share to labor in the production of goods was disproportionately small. In a suit of clothes, for instance, it was said, selling at wholesale for $8, and retailing for $10, the contractor received little more than a dollar, out of which he had to pay his help, while the material used did not cost over half the wholesale price.

Concretely put, the demands of the striking workers in respect to wages were for a general 20 per cent increase, to be apportioned as follows: for machine cutters, knife cutters, and cloth markers, $25; for trimmers, $22; for lining cutters, $20; for bushelmen and examiners, $18; for operatives of the first class (that is, those who sewed around coats, sewed in sleeves, and made pockets), $25; for operatives of the second class (that is, those who marked lining, and who stitched collars and coats), $22; for operatives of the third class (that is, those who made sleeves, and all others who worked at the machine), $16; for tailors of the first class (that is, shapers, underbasters, and fitters), $24; for tailors of the second class (that is, edge basters, canvass basters, collar makers, lining basters, and bushelmen), $21; for tailors of the third class (that is, armhole basters, sleeve makers, and similar workers), $17; for pressers, who were also bushelmen, $24; for regular pressers of the second class, $24; for underpressers and edge-pressers, $18; for women and children workers, who were button-sewers and bushel hands, $12; for hand button hole makers of the first class, 3½ cents per hole; for workers on sack coats, 2½ cents per hole; and for fellers, not less than $10 a week.

In respect to hours of work, there was a formal demand for the 48-hour week, though it was quite understood that the workers would be well satisfied for the present if they could obtain 50 or 52 hours. For work overtime, pay at the rate of time and half was asked, and for holidays double time. In addition, there was demanded the abolition of the system of fining, of charges for power, breakage, etc., and of subcontracting, including tenement house work. The question of the recognition of the union was not raised as a direct issue; and while it was hoped that the employers would treat with their employees through the union, it was felt that the time was not opportune to insist upon this point.

As the time approached for the strike the employers were not in ignorance as to what was to happen. They said afterwards that many of the strikers left without warning, but there were really few of the manufacturers who did not expect the strike. Not a large number of the men, however, presented a formal statement of their demands on leaving, it being claimed on the part of the workers that it was understood that all offers of settlement should be presented to the regular settlement committee of the union.

The manufacturers averred that they were quite willing to listen to the complaints of the workers, but that such complaints should come from them individually. They expressed a desire to make all the shops sanitary, and to remedy other abuses. As to changes in the hours of labor and the rates of wages, they declared that these were beyond their control, being regulated for the most part by the competition of other cities. Already they were paying, so they said, higher wages than prevailed in other places. If the present wage demands were granted, they alleged, the cost to the public would be increased one-third. Indeed, a trade paper[8] stated that one of the reasons for the firm stand of the manufacturers was to keep the price of ready-made clothing from rising to too great a height. Finally, they argued, they might be disposed to grant some of the demands after consideration, but this would have to come later, as their orders had been taken on the present basis.

Though the beginning of the strike was set for the last day of the old year, it was understood by the workers when they left the shops on the Saturday before, December 28, that they would not return to work. To the first call the great majority of the workers, perhaps three-fourths, responded. These were added to the following days, and by the second week probably from 80 to 85 per cent of the workers had left the shops; while perhaps four hundred shops in all were affected. Some of the manufacturers claimed to have a fair number at work still during the strike, while a small number of strike-breakers were induced to enter. However, in respect to the great number of the shops, there was very little work carried on, the employers contenting themselves with disposing of the goods already in stock. The industry was in fact almost entirely tied up.

The battle was now on. On the one side were the workers, some in the various locals of the United Workers of America, and some outside the unions, but standing with them. A dozen or so different nationalities were represented. The Jews formed much the largest section, furnishing over half of the number. The Italians came next, with perhaps a third. The remainder were Germans, Poles, Russians, Americans, and others. A part of the strikers, perhaps a third, were women. It is to be noted that the makers of made-to-order clothing, unless in connection with some factory, did not participate in the strike. They are mainly the so-called "two-room" tailors, found in such numbers over the city, who work independently, and usually alone, though sometimes calling in an assistant.

[8] *Clothier and Furnisher,* March, 1913.

On the other side were the manufacturers. They were themselves split into several groups. The manufacturers of the better grade clothing were composed of four bodies: the New York Clothing Trade Association, the Tailors to the Trade, the Association of Boys' Clothing Manufacturers of Greater New York, and the Association of Clothing Manufacturers. During the strike they were banded together in the Allied Clothing Trades. They comprised over two hundred manufacturers, and employed about a fifth of the workers. At the beginning it was claimed that they had 90 per cent of the trade, though this was later proved far from being the case. The next large organization of manufacturers was the United Merchant and Manufacturers Association, with a very large business. Below them were a large number of smaller associations, and at the bottom a considerable group of modest individual establishments. In addition, a very important factor was found in the United Association of Clothing Contractors, composed of some 2,000 concerns, which claimed to have over three-fourths of the workers, and over half of the work.

Hardly had the strike commenced, however, when efforts were made for its settlement. The Committee on Arbitration of the Chamber of Commerce offered its services the very day the strike was called. It proposed an investigation of conditions in New York and other cities, the workers to return to work pending the investigation. To this suggestion the manufacturers were quite agreeable. But by the workers it was rejected on the ground that they had no assurance of the employers' acceptance of the plan in case it should prove adverse to them. It was also felt by them that in the return of the workers to the shops all the great tactical advantages in the organization of the strike would at once be lost. The employers thereupon, declaring that they washed their hands of responsibility for the continuance of the strike, announced that they would have no more dealings with the unions.

Soon afterward new conferences began at the offices of the Bar Association, extending through most of the month of January. These were between the United Manufacturers and Merchants Association, the United Association of Clothing Contractors, and the United Garment Workers. The last named organization had previously declined to have anything to do with the contractors; but this body soon made plain the necessity of their participation in the arrangements, and if the negotiations had proceeded to an issue, they might have been a party in the final agreement. In proof of their good faith and of their strength, the contractors offered to put up a bond of $100,000 as security for the fulfillment of their obligations. No little encouragement towards the settling of the strike was presented by the United Manufacturers Association. Though ridiculed by the other manufacturers' organizations in the trade, it appeared an intelligent and progressive body. It indicated its thorough willingness to take part in collective bargaining with the workers, and, indeed, even to accept a protocol agreement on somewhat the same order as that adopted in the cloak, suit and skirt industry in 1910. After various discussions, however, the best that this body could offer was a 54-hour week, and an advance in wages of 5, 7½, and 10 per cent., according to the pay before the strike, but in no case to be less than one dollar a week. Though the officials of the union did not appear altogether opposed to this proposition, the workers made it clear that they would not be satisfied with it. Another offer was made of a general advance in wages of 10 per cent, with a further increase in the following April of 5 per cent, and of a 54-hour week for all but the cutters, who were to have 48; but the unions, with the exception of the cutters, who were rather disposed to look with favor upon the scheme, insisted upon a 20 per cent raise, or at least a 15 per cent immediate one, with a maximum of 50 hours a week. A compromise being acceptable to neither party, the negotiations were finally abandoned.

There were other efforts made to settle the strike, coming for the most part from groups of citizens, but few of these received serious consideration. The State Board of Mediation and Arbitration, the official public body which had been created to do what it could to adjust industrial disputes, also offered its services during the entire period of the strike. Its only accomplishments, however, were near the end, when it succeeded in effecting agreements between some of the smaller associations and their men. Once or twice it seemed that there might be a national investigation, several propositions to this end having been offered in Congress. Outside efforts were finally instrumental in bringing about a settlement, as we shall find, but these came when the men were virtually exhausted, and when it was seen that the time was ripe for successful intervention.

At the beginning of the strike the strikers had engaged a number of halls near the clothing districts, and here they settled down as best they could to the task of waiting. To many the strike bore hard. Savings soon melted away, dispossess notices became increasingly frequent, and clamors of wives and children grew louder and louder. Appeals for help began to crowd upon the leaders, and they were often pressed to devise means to meet the situation. Some help was received from friends, especially in the providing of food. Over ten thousand dollars came from the suit, cloak, and skirt unions. The one spectacular feature of the strike was a parade during its second week. In it there were over 50,000 marchers, who well indicated the cosmopolitan character of the workers. The parade was by the newspapers called "a model of order."

As a matter of fact, the strike was on the whole conducted with no great disorder or breach of the peace; and in view of the numbers involved, the amount of violence committed was small. In certain districts, especially in the Lafayette Street section and in Williamsburg and Brownsville, there were more or less frequent clashes between the strikers and the police, with numerous arrests.

It was proved during the strike that the officials of the Garments Workers' Union were of a conservative temperment. More than once they were charged with being over-eager to accept compromises which would not have been advantageous to the workers; and occasionally a revolt was even threatened. The radical element was very much of the same character as that which of late years has been making more and more determined efforts to guide the policy of the American Federation of Labor. This element, however, did not, in the present strike, find itself able to wrest the leadership from the conservative group, and the latter remained in control to the end.

During the continuance of the strike some bitterness was engendered among the strikers by the efforts of certain manufacturers to restrain the former from picketing, though in the end because of the course adopted by the court, no great harm resulted. Two weeks after the strike had begun, one of the largest firms applied for a blanket injunction against the picketing of the strikers, joined in soon after by nineteen other firms. The order asked for was a sweeping one, which was to forbid the strikers from "associating or loitering in front of or in the vicinity of the plaintiffs' places of business or from establishing or maintaining a system of picketing by stationing or keeping one or more pickets," etc. A temporary injunction was secured; but when it was sought to have the injunction made permanent, the court declared that it could not be granted on an *ex parte* hearing, but only as a question of fact on the appearance of both sides. Before the matter was finally determined, the strike had come to an end, and the injunction proceedings were allowed to drop.

The strike was broken almost from the start by settlements with individual firms. Few days passed without there being some agreement effected of greater or less extent, and the consequent return of a body of workers, numbering sometimes several thousand, to the shops. The largest settlement was with the Canal Street Clothing Association in the middle of February, in which an agreement was signed allowing an increase in wages of from 10 to 20 per cent, with a week of 54 hours, to be later reduced. In this settlement some 10,000 persons were affected. By the third week in February about 40,000 workers were said to have returned to their shops. Towards the end of the month settlements were being rapidly effected with the boys' clothing manufacturers especially.

Finally, at the end of February, with half of the workers back in their shops, and with the strikers' resources all but exhausted, those still out were ready to consider settlements on a basis quite different from their original demands. The employers at the same time, under the burden of their heavy losses, were willing to make more or less substantial concessions to the strikers. Both sides had grown weary of the struggle, and were anxious to find some common meeting ground.

With the situation thus, the opportunity had arrived for outside parties to volunteer their good offices—something that had not been possible at an earlier stage. It was felt in particular that if the allied associations could be brought into an agreement with their workers, the rest of the manufacturers would speedily fall in line. Accordingly, on the last day of February a well-known citizen, himself formerly a clothing manufacturer, wrote to the leading spirit in the allied associations and asked what would be the best that the manufacturers would offer. After consultation, the following were presented as a basis of settlement, in all the terms of which the manufacturers for their part promised faithful compliance:

1. The strikers were to return to work at once.

2. The question of hours was to be left to the judgment of three well-known citizens, their recommendations to be binding, but to be made with reference to conditions in other cities.

3. A general increase in wages was to be made of one dollar a week, with a proportionate amount to piece workers, to take effect at once, with no reduction during dull times, while the wages of the cutters were to be determined specially between them and the manufacturers.

4. Proper sanitary conditions were to be guaranteed; subcontracting was to be abolished; contract shops were to have the same hours and conditions of work as the inside shops; and various minor abuses were to be remedied.

5. No discrimination was to be shown in the employment of workers with respect to their attitude at the time of the strike.

When this offer was received by the union officials, it was accepted without delay, and the strike was declared off by the Executive Committee. It was believed that it was the best that could be secured, and that to continue the strike would only mean added hardship. Most of the workers felt the same way, and indicated at once their willingness to return on these terms. However, there were a certain number, for the most part of the Brotherhood of Tailors, who declared that they would not have the agreement, and were for continuing the strike. They denounced the union officials for calling it off, charging them with having effected the agreement without first submitting it to the workers, and with knowing little of the foreign elements and their demands. These insurgents numbered less than 10,000, and after a week decided that they could gain little over the terms offered, whereupon they too fell in.

Within two weeks after the close of the strike, the committee appointed to investigate the hours of labor in other cities, reported. It had examined the conditions in Philadelphia, Baltimore, Boston, and Chicago. It made note of the general tendency to shorten hours, and the discontent with 54 or more hours in the clothing trade, and recognized the position of New York as leader in the trade. It accordingly advised 53 hours as the proper number per week, which after January 1, 1914, should be further reduced to 52. The hours for cutters were not so much affected, being in some cases 50, and in others 48.

The strike was now at an end. The shops were soon running on full time, and even more briskly than before the strike to make up for lost time. The workers, after their long fight, had won only a part of what they had asked for, though some of these gains were quite substantial. In all their specific demands they had secured some concessions, and in those respecting material conditions had obtained nearly all they had asked. The keenest matter of regret was in the failure to obtain the full increase in wages which had been desired, although it is not impossible that those actually secured were all that many of the workers seriously expected.

The manufacturers, on their side, pointed out with a certain amount of truth that they had been willing to grant many of these concessions from the very first, and that the workers had accomplished no great gains by holding out as they did. On the whole, however, it appears that the workers did secure concessions from their prolongation of the strike that would have been impossible earlier. This is notably true in respect to the matter of hours. It was no light thing to obtain first 53 hours, and later 52, in an industry where 56 hours or more had been no unusual practice.[9]

In the strike no such victory had been won as had been the case in the cloak, suit and skirt industry in 1910, when, after a hard struggle of nine weeks, there had been secured a 25 per cent increase in wages, a reduction of hours to 49 a week, and the preferential shop, under the protocol agreement. In the strike of 1913 such results were impossible of accomplishment. The workers in the men's garment industry were of too varied a complexion to have a thoroughly cohesive organization. A large number were raw immigrants, many of whom were in the lowest scale of employment and seldom far removed from destitution, and who could be expected to have little apprecia-

[9] Simultaneously with, or occurring soon after, the New York strike, were strikes in the men's garment industry in Boston, Philadelphia, Rochester, Chicago, Baltimore, and other cities, in nearly all of which reductions of hours were secured.

tion of the benefits of a union. The garment workers were thus not able long to pit their resources against those of the employers.

There is today in the industry a somewhat stronger union than existed before the strike. Yet the difficulties in building up a powerful and lasting organization in the entire industry remain. There has been a certain increase in membership in the unions, but on the whole not a particularly large permanent addition. It should not be thought, nevertheless, that the strike bore no fruit in the way of enhancing esteem for unions. The moral effect could not be wholly absent, and most of the workers probably realize the strength to be found in organization to a greater degree than was possible before the strike.[10]

In the final settlement of the strike a consideration not to be lost sight of was the introduction of the principle of arbitration, and this is to be regarded as a not unimportant gain to the workers. It had been suggested from the beginning, as we have seen; but coming when it did it probably secured more far-reaching results than would otherwise have been possible.

Yet to the public it must remain a matter of deep regret that the principle of arbitration and mutual concession could not have had application sooner. Though there were public agencies whose business it was to deal with such affairs, and though there were offers from private bodies to help adjust the difficulties, no suggestion was listened to till both sides were weakened, and one was exhausted. No external pressure was allowed to influence either combatant. The public could do nothing but look on, and await the conclusion. The economic waste was great—the pecuniary loss to the employers, the suffering and privation to the workers and their families, the inconvenience and injury to the public. In the end no real issue was determined, and no advance was made in settling industrial disputes or improving industrial relations. For such a strike the price paid was too heavy a one.

---

[10] The President of the United Garment Workers states that since the strike has occurred, "there is a growing tendency on the part of the manufacturers to treat with our unions through accredited representatives." *American Federationist*, Sept., 1913.

DO NOT REMOVE
OR
MUTILATE CARD

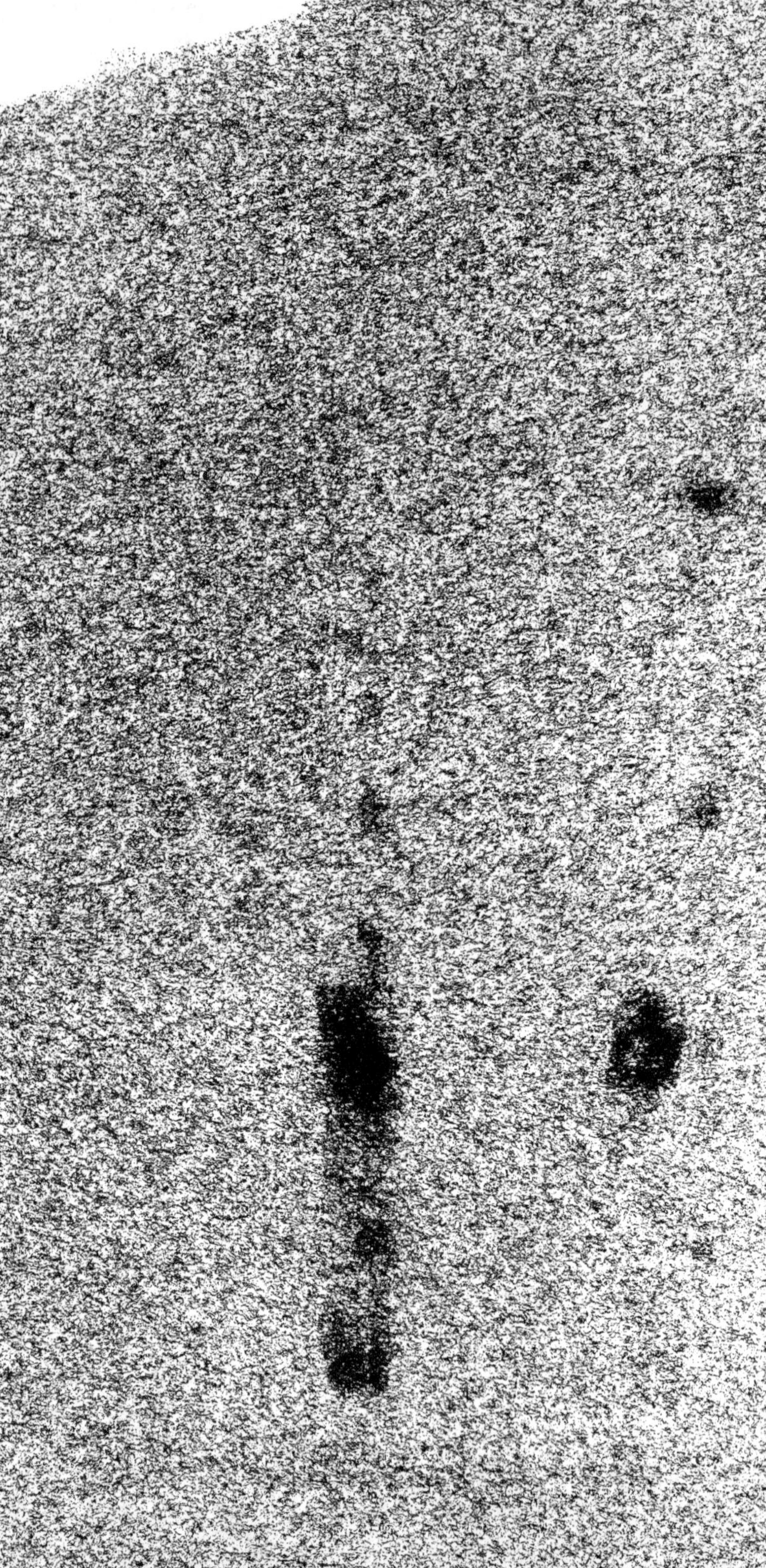

www.ingramcontent.com/pod-product-compliance
Lightning Source LLC
LaVergne TN
LVHW011134110826
845150LV00008B/2334

* 9 7 8 1 4 1 8 1 9 4 6 7 3 *